Tropical North Queensland

Ric J. Steininger

photographic artist

"An impression of the Tropical North"

Produced by:

Ric J. Steininger - Publications Pty Ltd

ABN: 34 335 605 933

Post: PO Box 12269, Cairns DC, Queensland 4870 Australia

Tel: 07 4052 1533 (int. +617 4052 1533)

Email: ric@steininger.com.au, **Web:** www.steininger.com.au

Ric J. Steininger - Gallery

Cairns, Australia
Lahaina, Maui USA

or visit my website on: **www.steininger.com.au**

Panoramic photography, design and published by Ric J. Steininger
Underwater photography by Stuart Ireland & Lisa Conyers

Published July 2004, reprinted 2005, 2009. Reprinted and revised 2014.

Copyright © 1992 - 2014 Ric J. Steininger & Calypso Productions

ISBN 0-9581633-1-6 **All rights reserved**

Printed in China by Everbest Printing Company Ltd

"Welcome to my gallery"

An Introduction

I take great pleasure in presenting my second book in the Impressions series; "Impressions of Cairns". This edition showcases a superb collection of special places in Tropical North Queensland.

I have been living here in Cairns for the past 18 years and have come to call it home. I love the life here and as the visitor that I once was, I wish to share with you some of the classic scenes, beauty and character of the region. These images are only an enticement, an impression of the Tropical North. There is so much more to explore. Many of the wonderful places captured in this book are only a very short drive from the heart of the city of Cairns. I hope this book inspires you to spend some time in this great place that I call home, Cairns, a city and an area treasured by all of us who live here.

All the panoramic photographs in this book were captured using an extremely large format panoramic camera. It is a traditional film based camera that is cumbersome and tedious to use. It is far from convenient to use compared to 35mm or digital cameras. And there is nothing instant about its use. The exposures tend to be very long and require heavy tripods and days of waiting. My aim is to master the challenge of capturing something truly special, then to bring the inspiration

of the great outdoors, indoors. Only a camera like this can bring the lifelike size into a room.

I have been working as a photographic artist for over twenty years using this wide panoramic camera as my canvas, and the natural light as my paint and brush. I call myself an artist; for the camera is just the medium that is used to capture my art. My gallery is Cairns' first photographic gallery, opening in 1997 and I have been proud to display these images that mean so much to me. I hope that they inspire you as much as they have been an inspiration to me ...

Ric J. Steininger

"Just another day at work!"

City of Cairns

A fine day looking over the special city of Cairns and surroundings, nestled at the base of rainforest covered mountains.

The Lagoon

A man made beach with water that reaches out to the ocean and beyond. A great place to spend time with family and friends.

The Esplanade

A very popular early morning walk on the Cairns Esplanade. The Esplanade is enjoyed by visitors and residents alike the whole day long.

The Pink House

A classical farmer's Queenslander house set amongst sugar cane ready for harvest.

Green Island

A popular coral Island off the coast of Cairns. Coral reefs islands are simply paradise for all who visit. With shady palm trees, white sand beaches and snorkelling in the aqua waters amongst the variety of tropical coral fish and turtles.

"Angel"

Off the coast of Cairns is Michaelmas Cay; a natural bird sanctuary in the middle of the Great Barrier Reef.

"Just Paradise!"

The sand cays situated off the coast of Cairns are spectacular natural wonders that are loved by all who have visited them.

Little Upolu

The crystal clear aqua waters sparkle in the sunlight. Sand cays off the coast of Cairns are a beautiful dream place to visit.

Dive Pontoons

A very safe and popular way to visit the reef is to come to one of these pontoons that are anchored like man-made islands next to coral reefs. Great for the professional diver or the first time snorkeler.

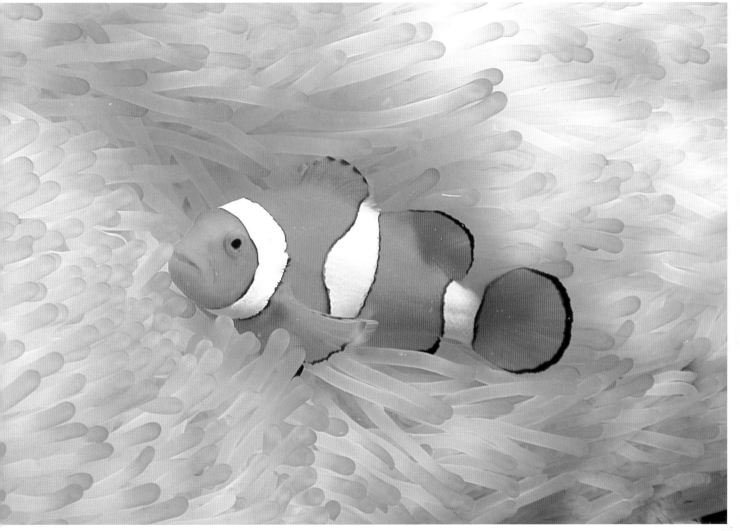

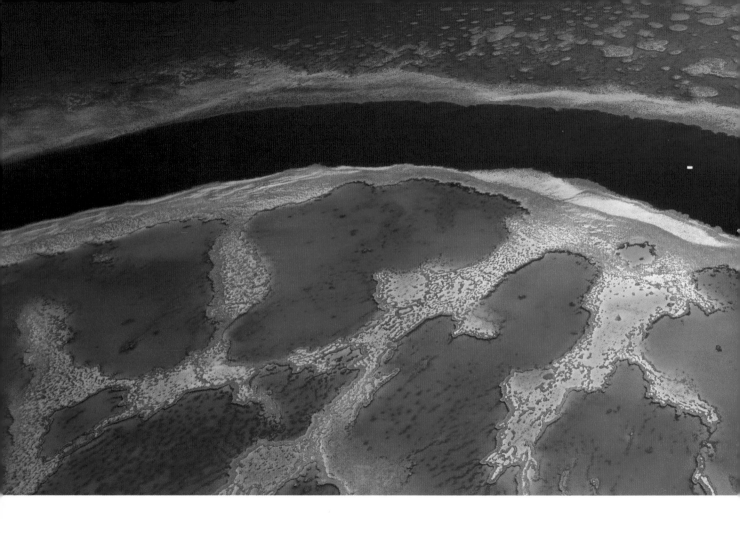

Great Reef
The Great Barrier Reef is a a living aquarium stretching 2300km long. It is the largest reef area in the world.

Palm Cove

Palm Cove is a quiet luxury beach resort town with Double Islands off its coast. Captured here in the calm of early morning.

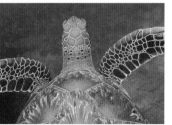

Palm Cove Sunrise

One of the most beautiful destinations in North Queensland ... Palm Cove at sunrise.

Ellis Beach

A classic Tropical North beach and coastline, with coconut palm trees and calm seas.

Kuranda Train

Climbing into the mountains, passing a number of waterfalls; with great views, especially that of Barron Gorge.

Barron Falls

Captured during the wet season after heavy rain; the roar of the water is deafening with the mist in the air and the roar of the falls reverberating through your chest. Can be visited by Kuranda Train or Skyrail *(left)*.

Millaa Millaa

Millaa Millaa Falls is one of the most photogenic waterfalls in the world; it is almost like a picture perfect fairy tale.

4 Mile Beach

The ocean of Tropical North Queensland has such a serenity and stillness that is unique and special to this area.

Low Isles

Low Isles is a classic coral island with it's clear white sand and coral reef. It also has a mangrove island that lies close by. The mountains behind Port Douglas can be clearly seen in the distance as you snorkel amongst coral and sea life.

St. Mary's by the Sea

The perfect setting for a tropical church, overlooking a small sheltered beach at Port Douglas.

Mossman

An attempt to capture the full life and energy of this powerful river; with soft warm light, huge boulders and powerful rapids.

Cape Tribulation

Crossing the Daintree River on one of Australia's only river ferries you enter an untouched rainforest experience. Pristine creeks flow all year around *(next page)*. *(right)* A perfect example of where the rainforest meets the sea.

Rainforest Creek

A perfectly pristine creek photographed in the rain, the waters rising and lightly flooding the small ferns.

Green Tree frog

Ulysses butterfly

Crocodile photo by: D'Arcy of Daintree 4WD

Crocodiles,
Kangaroos
&
Koalas

Cassowary

Native to Tropical North Queensland they are crucial to the region's rainforest. Eating the brightly coloured berries and fruit they are the only means for many species of trees to spread their seeds. It is as though the very colours of the fruit they eat are displayed in their necks and facial feathers. Even their eggs can show the similar variations of colours.

www.steininger.com.au

Photography is a medium of formidable
contradictions - it is ridiculously easy
and impossibly difficult.

Edward Steichen (1879 - 1973)

Books by Ric J. Steininger in his Impression series are:

IMPRESSIONS OF AUSTRALIA
Featuring images from around Australia.

IMPRESSIONS OF CAIRNS
Featuring images from Cairns and surrounding areas; including Reef, rainforest and animals.

IMPRESSIONS OF THE GREAT BARRIER REEF
Featuring images from the Great Barrier Reef including above and below water.